Why we love cupcakes

You will love decorating these little cupcakes. Bright, cheerful and fun, they are the perfect centrepiece for your party. Many are simple enough for children to have a go, and there is a design to suit absolutely any occasion.

You can make the little sugarpaste models weeks or months in advance, ready to finish your cupcakes, just remember not to store them anywhere damp.

Change the colours and mix and match the little models to create your own original designs, and have lots and lots of fun!

1

2

3

4

Contents

5

6

7

8

Crafty Cupcakes

ANN PICKARD

Crafty Cupcakes

THE GUILD OF MASTER CRAFTSMAN PUBLICATIONS

To all my lovely family, especially my Mum.

First published 2012 by
Guild of Master Craftsman Publications Ltd
Castle Place, 166 High Street, Lewes,
East Sussex BN7 1XU

Text © Ann Pickard, 2012
Copyright in the Work © GMC Publications Ltd, 2012

ISBN 978-1-86108-853-6

A catalogue record for this book is available from
the British Library.

Publisher: Jonathan Bailey
Production Manager: Jim Bulley
Managing Editor: Gerrie Purcell
Senior Project Editor: Virginia Brehaut
Copy Editor: Kathy Steer
Managing Art Editor: Gilda Pacitti

Step-by-step photography by Anthony Bailey
All other photography by Gilda Pacitti

Set in Gill Sans
Colour origination by GMC Reprographics
Printed and bound in China by C&C Offset Ltd

9

10

11

12

13

14

15

16

17

18

19

20

21

22

23

24

25

26

27

28

29

30

No one could resist this little duck swimming around in the pond. You could add some tiny ducklings to keep her company or make her in different coloured icing.

Duck pond

Materials

Yellow, red and grey sugarpaste (see pages 138–39)

Turquoise and green royal icing (see page 149)

No. 9 modelling tool

Black paste food colour

Piping bags (see pages 144–45)

Cocktail stick or toothpick

Pearl lustre spray

Palette knife

Part	Template	Colour
Body	Small D	Yellow
Head	E	Yellow
Beak	I	Red

See templates for sizes on page 132

1 Body Form the body into a teardrop shape with a nice point at the end. Place it on its side and bend the point upwards for the tail.

2 Head Make a perfect little round head for the duck from a ball of yellow sugarpaste.

3 Attach head Stick the head to the fat end of the duck's body. If it doesn't stay by itself, use a little brushed-on water. Make a hole in the middle of it ready for the beak.

4 Beak Form the beak into a sausage shape with a point at both ends. Push one point into the hole in the head. The beak needs to be pointing upwards so that the duck looks cheerful.

5 Eyes Mark two long eyes (see 'How to mark eyes', page 143) on the duck's face with black paste colour and a cocktail stick (or toothpick).

6 Pebbles Mix up a ball of marbled grey sugarpaste. Pull off little pieces and form tiny pebbles of various sizes.

7 Pond Cover the top of your cupcake with a generous quantity of turquoise royal icing. Using a palette knife, shape it into a swirl at the top.

8 Add duck Place the little duck in the centre of your pond, immediately after covering with the royal icing 'water' and she will stick firmly in place.

9 Arrange pebbles Start to arrange the little grey pebbles around the edge of the blue royal icing. If you don't want to pipe the grass (see step 10), you can put pebbles all around the outside of the pond.

10 Grass Half fill a small piping bag with green royal icing (see page 145) and pipe some stalks of grass around the edge of the pond. Spray with pearl lustre spray for shimmer on the water.

Spring has arrived, and this pretty little bluebird is keeping her eggs warm in her chocolate nest. This would make a lovely design for an Easter or spring cake.

Bird's nest

Materials

Marbled brown, blue, white and black sugarpaste
 (see pages 138–39) or chocolate
 buttercream (see page 148)
Blue royal icing (see page 149)
No. 9 modelling tool
Large heart cutter
Medium heart cutter
Piece of uncooked spaghetti
Pair of nail scissors

Part	Template	Colour
Nest	B	Marbled brown
Body	D	Blue
Head	E	Blue
Beak	H	Black
Eggs	2 × F	White

See templates for sizes on page 132

1 Cover cupcake Cover the top of your cupcake with a disc of sugarpaste in marbled brown (see page 142) or cover with chocolate buttercream (see page 148).

2 Nest Roll the ball of sugarpaste to a length of 6in (150mm) curled around on itself.

3 Add nest Place the nest on top of the cupcake, then using a small pair of nail scissors, start to snip the outside edge of the nest. Work all the way around and then do two more irregular lines inside.

4 Eggs Shape the two little white balls into oval eggs and place them into the nest.

5 Body Form the blue body of the bird into a flat cone shape. Push a piece of uncooked spaghetti in ready to stick the head on.

6 Head Take the blue ball for the head, then place firmly onto the spaghetti and make a big hole in the middle with the pointed end of a modelling tool.

7 Beak eyes and feathers
Shape a little black beak with a sharp point at both ends, then push one end into the hole until it is secure. Mark the eyes (see 'How to mark eyes', page 143) with black paste colour and a cocktail stick (or toothpick). Scratch some marks over the breast area to represent feathers.

8 Wings Roll out some blue sugarpaste, ⅛in (2–3mm) thick. Cut out a large heart 1½in (35mm) across, cut it in half, and mark lines along it then cut the tips off.

9 Tail Cut a smaller heart ⅘in (20mm) across. Mark lines all along it with a knife blade, then cut the tip off the heart.

10 Attaching wings and tail
Stick the wings and the tail to the bird with a little blue royal icing, allowing them all to slope outwards, resting on the nest edge.

No need to make all the bunny, just have his little head popping out of this springtime cake. Instead of the flowers, you could make little orange icing carrots to place around him.

Bunny rabbit

Materials

Dark brown, green, medium brown and yellow sugarpaste
   (see pages 138–39)

Green and red royal icing (see page 149)

Apricot purée (see page 149)

Piping bag (see pages 144–5)

Small blossom cutter

Black paste food colour

Cocktail stick or toothpick

Part	Template	Colour
Hole	E	Dark brown
Head	Small D	Medium brown
Nose	I	Dark brown
Feet	2 x G	Medium brown

See templates for sizes on page 132

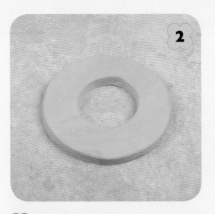

1 **Cover cupcake** Brush the cake with apricot purée. Squash a ball of dark brown sugarpaste quite flat, and place in the centre of the cupcake.

2 **Cut out circle** Roll out a circle of green sugarpaste the same size as the top of the cupcake, then cut out a 1in (25mm) circle from the centre.

3 **Attach circle** Stick this shape on top of the cupcake, pressing firmly down on to the purée to stick in place.

4 **Head** Form the medium brown ball for the head into a long pointy cone shape, then cut the pointed end halfway down and divide equally as shown above.

5 **Ears** Pull the tips of the ears outwards; mark a line with a knife down each ear; and three more lines across the bottom of the face, crossing in the centre. Push a hole into the centre ready for the nose.

6 **Nose** Shape the little dark brown ball into a teardrop for the nose. Push the point of the teardrop into the face and flatten slightly.

7 **Eyes and feet** Mark the eyes (see 'How to mark eyes', page 143). Form two little medium brown balls into teardrop shapes for the feet.

8 **Attach feet and head** Stick the feet on top of the cupcake with the points over the dark brown hole and the rounded ends pointing outwards, and pop on the head covering the back of the feet.

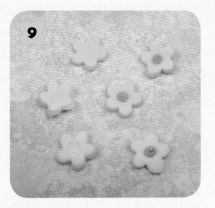

9 **Flowers** Roll out some yellow sugarpaste to a ¹⁄₁₂in (2mm) thickness. Cut lots of little blossoms and push a rounded shaped tool into the centre to cup them. Pipe a red ball in the centre of each one with red royal icing.

10 **Grass** Pipe some green grass around the edges of your cupcake and also around the rabbit hole (see page 145). Use a little green icing to stick the flowers in place.

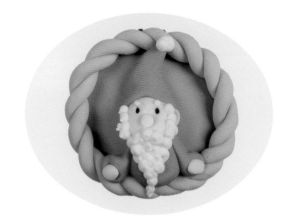

This festive little Santa Claus resembles Christmas decorations that hang from the tree. You could also make some with snowmen inside the twisted wreath.

Santa Claus

Materials

Green, red, peach and light 'teddy bear' brown sugarpaste
  (see pages 138–39)

White royal icing (see page 149)

Apricot purée (see page 149)

No. 9 modelling tool

Black paste food colour

Cocktail stick or toothpick

Piping bags (see pages 144–45)

No. 42 small star piping tube

Part	Template	Colour
Head	D	Peach
Body	E	Red
Nose	H	Peach
Rope	2 × D	Teddy bear brown
Hat	Small D	Red
Arms	F	Red
Hands	Large H	Peach

See templates for sizes on page 132

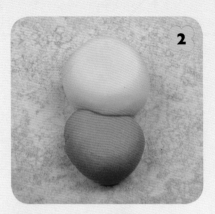

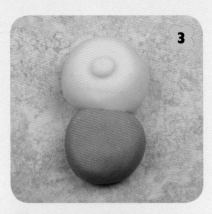

1 Cover cupcake Cover the top of your cupcake with a disc of sugarpaste in green (see page 142). Your cake can be flat or slightly domed for this design (see page 141).

2 Body and head Form the body from the ball of red sugarpaste and the head from the ball of peach sugarpaste, which slightly overlaps it.

3 Nose Form the ball for the nose into a teardrop shape and push the pointed end into a hole in the head.

4 Hat Form the hat into a long pointy cone shape. Curve the bottom of the hat up in the middle and stick on his head with a little brushed-on water to secure. Bend the top point sideways a little.

5 Rope Roll out two thin sausages of light teddy bear brown sugarpaste for the rope, about 9in (23cm) long. Twist them around each other tightly starting from the centre.

6 **Attach rope** Brush apricot purée around the outer edge of the cupcake and stick the rope in place, joining the ends by cutting diagonally. Stick Santa inside and mark his ears with the end of the modelling tool.

7 **Attach arms** Add the arms, each one is a little teardrop shape 1in (25mm) long. Stick them to the sides of the body with a little brushed-on water to secure, and position the ends of the arms over the rope.

8 **Hands** Push a hole up into the end of each arm and form two teardrop-shaped hands. Push the point of each teardrop up the end of a sleeve and squash the hands down slightly on to the rope.

9 **Eyes and beard** Mark the eyes (see 'How to mark eyes, page 143) with black paste colour. Half fill a piping bag with royal icing and a No. 42 piping tube and pipe the beard from lots of joined up stars.

10 **Bobble** As a finishing touch, pipe a tiny dot above each eye and give him a bobble at the top of his hat.

Who could resist this little Christmas tree cupcake? As an alternative, make a white tree on a blue background for a sophisticated look. Little stars could be added to the decorations for a more dressed tree.

Christmas tree

Materials

Red, white and green sugarpaste (see pages 138–39)

White royal icing (see page 149)

Piping bag (see pages 144–45)

No. 42 small star piping tube

Silver dragées (balls)

Pair of nail scissors

Part	Template	Colour
Pot	C	Red
Tree	B	Green

See templates for sizes on page 132

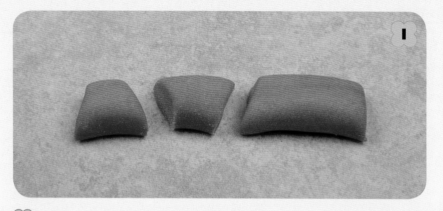

1 Pots Roll out a sausage 2½in (70mm) long from the red sugarpaste and cut out four pots for your Christmas trees.

2 Add lines Mark each pot with three or four lines before placing it on your cupcake.

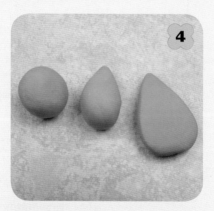

3 Add pot Cover the top of your cupcake with a disc of white sugarpaste (see page 142), then stick on the pot with a little brushed-on water.

4 Shape tree Form the little ball of green sugarpaste for the tree into a cone shape, then flatten it.

5 Tree Slice the bottom off the Christmas tree in a straight line and discard the cut-off piece to use again.

6 Shaping branches Using a pair of small nail scissors, start to cut the branches. Open the blades, rest them against the tree pointing upwards and make a deep cut.

7 Finishing branches Work carefully from the top of the tree downwards and finish around the base with four or five cuts.

8 Attach tree Use a little brushed-on water to stick the tree on to your cake touching the red pot.

9 Decorate tree Using small silver dragées, decorate the tree. Push them firmly into the green icing while it is still soft, and they will stay in place.

10 Decorate cupcake Place a small star tube into your paper piping bag and half fill with white royal icing, then pipe little white blobs all around the outer edge of the cupcake. For royal icing tips and piping techniques see page 146.

The snowman is such fun to make and easy enough for children to have a go at. Make the model in advance to keep the pressure off you at Christmas. Sprinkle with some icing sugar for a more snowy backdrop.

Snowman

Materials

White, dark blue, orange and light blue sugarpaste
  (see pages 138–39)
White royal icing (see page 149)
No. 9 modelling tool
Piping bag (see pages 144–45)
Black paste food colour
Cocktail stick or toothpick
Pearl lustre spray
Paintbrush
Piece of uncooked spaghetti

Part	Template	Colour
Body	C	White
Arms	2 x F	White
Scarf	F	Dark blue
Head	D	White
Nose	G	Orange

See templates for sizes on page 132

1 Body Form a cone-shaped body with the ball of white sugarpaste, about 1⅛in (30mm) high.

2 Arms Make the two little balls into teardrop shapes, ⅘in (20mm) long for the arms. Stick one to the side of the body, using a little water to secure if necessary.

3 Attach arms Join the second arm to the other side of the body, ensure that the points meet at the top, and stick the arms down well.

4 Scarf Slightly squash the ball of dark blue sugarpaste and place it right on top of the body where the tops of the arms meet for the scarf.

5 Head Form the white sugarpaste head, then push a piece of spaghetti down into the body and place the head on top.

6 Nose Make a hole in the middle of the snowman's face. Form an orange carrot nose by making a shape with a point at both ends (see Duck's beak, page 12). Push one point into the hole and make little lines all the way down it.

7 Eyes Give the snowman two long friendly eyes (see 'How to mark eyes', page 143) using the black paste colour and a cocktail stick (or toothpick).

8 Cover cupcake Cover the top of your cupcake with a light blue sugarpaste disc and spray it all over with pearl lustre spray.

9 Attach snowman Pop the snowman on to the cake, sticking with royal icing. Half fill a small piping bag with white royal icing, cut a small straight hole off the end of the bag and pipe a few little dots of white icing.

10 Snowflakes Continue piping until you have snowflakes all over the top of the cake in a variety of sizes.

Make a really high cupcake and turn it into a domed icy igloo for this cute little penguin to perch on. He has snowballs at the ready to play with his friends.

Penguin

Materials

White, orange and black sugarpaste (see pages 138–39)

Filling cream or apricot purée (see pages 148–49)

No. 9 modelling tool

Black paste food colour

Cocktail stick or toothpick

Paintbrush

Rolling pin

Icing sugar

Part	Template	Colour
Body	Small D	White
Feet	2 x G	Orange
Beak	H	Orange

See templates for sizes on page 132

1 Body and feet Form the ball for the body into a cone shape with a slightly rounded top 1in (25mm) high. The two orange feet are teardrop shapes, stick them side by side.

2 Attach feet Pick up the body and place it firmly down on to the back of the orange feet. Slide the penguin forwards on your work surface and the feet will attach themselves.

3 Mark toes Use the pointed end of your modelling tool to make three impressions on each of the feet, as you push the tool in, press down and the feet will spread out.

4 Beak Make a big hole in the body a third of the way down. Form the ball for the beak into a double-pointed shape.

5 Add beak Firmly push one point of the beak into the hole in the face. If it falls out, make the hole a little bigger and try again.

6 Back Dust your work surface with a little icing sugar and roll out a piece of black sugarpaste to a thickness of ⅛in (2–3mm), then cut the penguin's back the size shown on page 151.

7 Stick on back Pick up the black triangle and brush off any excess icing sugar. Brush a little water down the middle of it and stick it to the back of the penguin with the point folding over the top of his head.

8 Cover cupcake Brush the top of your cake with apricot purée or spread thinly with filling cream. Stick on a disc of white sugarpaste ⅕in (5mm) thick and large enough to cover it completely. Rub the surface gently with your palm to smooth it.

9 Igloo Using the tip of your knife, start to mark the blocks of the igloo into the white surface, and continue until they are marked all over.

10 Snowballs Stick your little penguin in place on top of his igloo and form some small white snowballs from sugarpaste to place next to him.

This little ghost wouldn't scare anyone, but the cakes would look fantastic at your Halloween party. For extra effect, colour your cupcake mixture green and add some chocolate chips to it.

Ghost

Materials

Orange, green and white sugarpaste (see pages 138–39)

No. 9 modelling tool

Black paste food colour

Cocktail stick or toothpick

Paintbrush

Pearl lustre spray

Part	Template	Colour
Ghost	B	White
Stalk	Large E	Green

See templates for sizes on page 132

1 Pumpkin Cover the top of your cupcake with a disc of orange sugarpaste ⅛in (4–5mm) thick (see page 142).

2 Mark lines Mark five curved lines on top of the cupcake with the back of a knife or the point of a modelling tool.

3 Hole for stalk Using the pointed end of the modelling tool, make a really deep and wide hole at the top of the pumpkin shape.

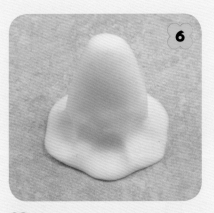

4 Stalk Form the green sugarpaste into a stalk and make long lines down it with a sharp knife. Stick the stalk into the hole at the top of the pumpkin shape.

5 Ghost Start to make the ghost. Form the ball of white sugarpaste into a rounded cone shape 2in (50mm) high.

6 Skirt Using your thumb and index finger, pinch a skirt all around the base of the little ghost.

7 Arms Halfway up each side of the body, gently pinch out two arms.

8 Eyes Mark two large eyes (see 'How to mark eyes', page 143) with black paste colour and a cocktail stick (or toothpick). If they are too small, repeat until they are the correct size.

9 Mouth Make a really big oval hole for the mouth by dipping the end of a paintbrush into the black paste colour and pushing it into the face.

10 Make ghost shimmer Spray some pearl lustre spray on to your ghost to make him shimmer and stick him in place on top of the pumpkin with a little royal icing or brushed-on water to secure.

This wicked witch, in her starry sky, will be a great centrepiece at your spooky Halloween celebration. Remember to make her eyes round beady dots and her mouth downturned so that she looks nasty!

Witch

Materials

Black, light green and white sugarpaste (see pages 138–39)

Purple royal icing (see page 149)

Piping bag (see pages 144–45)

Small star cutter

Round cutters

Cocktail stick or toothpick

Paintbrush

Edible glitter (optional)

Part	Template	Colour
Face	C	Green
Nose	G	Green
Collar	F	Black

See templates for sizes on page 132

1 Cover cupcake Cover the top of your cupcake with a disc of black sugarpaste (see page 142).

2 Head Shape the witch's head into an oval, and squash it down slightly. Make a long pointy nose from a ball of green sugarpaste.

3 Facial features Place the head in position on the cake, and mark the ears with the rounded end of the modelling tool. Stick on the nose with a little brushed-on water and mark tiny beady eyes. (See 'How to mark eyes', page 143).

4 Collar Form the black collar into a sausage shape 1in (25mm) long. Cut the ends off straight and mark lines along it.

5 **Hat** Cut the pointed hat shape, using the template on page 151 as a guide. Cut a circle of black sugarpaste ⅛in (4mm) thick and 1½in (38mm) across, and slice it in half.

6 **Brim of hat** Stick the brim of the hat to the top of her head, and add the little curved collar that sits underneath her chin.

7 **Add hat** Using a little brushed-on water to secure, place the top of her pointy witch's hat above the brim.

8 **Mouth and hair** Paint on the mouth. Half fill a small piping bag with purple royal icing and pipe long strands of hair fanning out from her face (see page 145).

9 **Stars** Cut lots of little white stars from white sugarpaste ⅛in (2–3mm) thick. If you allow them to dry for a little while they will be easier to handle.

10 **Add stars** Complete your design by adding the stars around the witch in the black sky. You could sprinkle on some edible glitter for an extra special effect.

This lovely snake is quick and easy to make. If you are in a hurry leave off the spots to save time or, alternatively, paint on some extra stripes or zigzags.

Smiley snake

Materials

Yellow and green sugarpaste (see pages 138–39)

Red, blue and green royal icing (see page 149)

Piping bags (see pages 144–45)

Black paste food colour

Cocktail stick or toothpick

Red jelly sweet

Small knife

Paintbrush

Pair of nail scissors

Part	Template	Colour
Body	A	Yellow

See templates for sizes on page 132

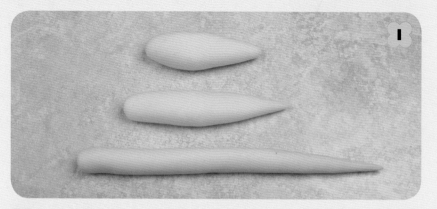

1 **Body** Form the body into a sausage shape 12in (300mm) long, and taper one end to a sharp point.

2 **Tail** Leaving the pointy tail showing at the base, curl the body around and upwards.

3 **Curl the body** Make each ring smaller as you go up and press them down so they stick together.

4 **Finish the body** Continue curling the body until the tail is across the front, and point the head forwards.

5 **Mouth** Using a small knife, gently slice an open mouth with one cut; hold the back of the head to support it as you make the cut. Lever the mouth open with the knife blade.

6 Facial features Using a pair of scissors or knife, cut a long thin pointed sliver off a red jelly sweet, then push it into the mouth, and stick with a little water if necessary. Mark two eyes (see 'How to mark eyes', page 143).

7 Cover cupcake Cover the top of your cupcake with a disc of bright green sugarpaste ⅓in (7–8mm) thick (see page 142). Snip it all around the outer edge with a pair of nail scissors, place your snake on top and stick with a little brushed-on water.

8 Red spots Fill a small piping bag with a little red royal icing, snip a small hole off the end, and start to pipe some red dots on your snake.

9 Blue spots Continue to pipe until they are widely spaced all over the snake, then repeat the steps using blue royal icing.

10 Green spots Finally, to finish your snake, add some green spots to make him look really colourful.

A great design to make for a cat lover. Change the colour of the cat to make it look like your pet! You can also make a marbled affect by mixing together a few colours of sugarpaste.

Cozy cat

Materials

Dark pink, black and white sugarpaste (see pages 138–39)

No. 9 modelling tool

Round cutters

Cocktail stick or toothpick

Part	Template	Colour
Feet	1 x F	Black
Body	C	Black
Head	Small D	Black
Nose	G	White
Nose tip	I	Pink
Tail	F	Black

See templates for sizes on page 132

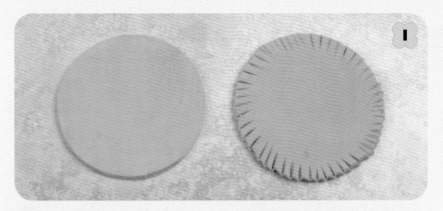

1 **Rug** Cut a disc in dark pink exactly the size of the top of your cupcake (see page 142). Before you cover the cupcake, mark little lines gently with a knife to make it look like the edge of a rug. Stick on top with filling cream or apricot purée.

2 **Mark rug and make feet** When it is in position, use your knife to make criss-cross lines over the top, then with the end of a cocktail stick (or toothpick) make lots of little dots at random. Form the feet from a ball of black sugarpaste into a sausage 1in (25mm) long, then bend it into a 'C' shape, and place on your cake, using brushed-on water to secure.

3 **Tail** The tail is a tapered sausage the same length as the feet but with a point at each end. Place it on the cake and use brushed-on water to secure.

4 **Body** Squash the round ball for the body and position it in the middle of the cake covering the end of the tail and the curve of the legs.

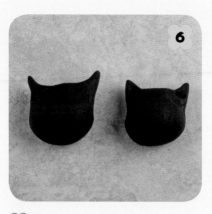

5 **Head** To make the head use your thumb and index finger to pinch two ears at the top of the ball. Flatten them slightly, and then pinch again.

6 **Ears** Use the pointed end of the modelling tool to press an indentation into both pointy ears.

7 **Face** Squash a ball of white sugarpaste and stick on to the centre of the cat's face, then blend the edges outwards and make a hole near the top ready for the nose.

8 **Nose and whiskers**
The small pink ball for the nose needs to be formed into a teardrop shape and the point inserted firmly into the hole, then flattened slightly. Mark three little lines for whiskers on each side of the nose with a knife.

9 **Add head** Join the cat's head to the body using a little brushed-on water to secure. Position it so that he is looking upwards and give him a little hole for a mouth.

10 **Eyes and fur** Mark your eyes (see 'How to mark eyes', page 143) using black paste colour. Finally, scratch on a furry effect using the end of a cocktail stick (or toothpick).

This cute dog could easily be adapted into a different breed by changing his ear shape or giving him spots or patches. You could also change the colour of his collar.

Cute dog

Materials

Green, 'teddy bear' brown, black sugarpaste
   (see pages 138–39)
No. 9 modelling tool
Round cutters
Black paste food colour
Cocktail stick or toothpick
Gold dragées (balls)
Icing sugar

Part	Template	Colour
Tail	G	Teddy bear brown
Feet	2 × G	Teddy bear brown
Head	C	Teddy bear brown
Ears	2 × F	Teddy bear brown
Collar	Small D	Black
Nose	Large H	Black

See templates for sizes on page 132

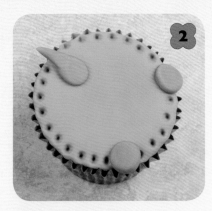

1 **Cover cupcake** Cover the top of the cupcake with a disc of green sugarpaste to seal the surface of the cake (see page 142). Using the pointed end of the modelling tool, push in holes all around the edge of the green cover.

2 **Feet and tail** In a triangle, stick on two round balls for feet and add a teardrop-shaped tail at the top, pointing outwards. Stick with a little brushed-on water if necessary.

3 **Body** Roll out some teddy bear brown sugarpaste on a surface dusted with icing sugar. Cut out a circle 1⅛in (45mm) wide and stick it on the cake.

4 **Collar** Form a ball of black sugarpaste for the collar, squash it flat, and then stick it in the centre of the dog's body.

5 **Head** Form the dog's head into a teardrop shape, and flatten it slightly.

6 **Add head** Using a little brushed-on water to secure, position the head on the body, ensuring that the collar is showing around the sides and above the head.

7 **Ears** Form a long teardrop shape from each ball of teddy-bear brown sugarpaste to make the ears. Flatten slightly and stick one on each side of the head. Pinch the bottom of the ears slightly outwards and make a hole ready for the nose.

8 **Nose** From a ball of black sugarpaste form a teardrop shape and push the point of the teardrop into the hole, make the hole bigger if it does not feel secure or fit inside.

9 **Facial features** Mark a little round hole for a mouth under the nose. Mark the eyes (see 'How to mark eyes', page 143) with black paste colour. Mark two tiny dots for the eyebrows too.

10 **Studs** While the black collar is still soft, push the gold dragées in firmly to make a lovely studded collar.

This lion cupcake would be perfect for a jungle or zoo-themed party. Make a selection of different animals in bright cases for a really colourful centrepiece.

Lion

Materials

Bright yellow, pale yellow/gold and black sugarpaste
   (see pages 138–39)

No. 9 modelling tool

Large sunflower or daisy cutter

Black paste food colour

Cocktail stick or toothpick

Paintbrush

Icing sugar

Part	Template	Colour
Head	C	Pale yellow/gold
Ears	2 x G	Pale yellow/gold
Nose	H	Black

See templates for sizes on page 132

1 Cover cupcake Cover the top of your cupcake with a disc of bright yellow sugarpaste (see page 142).

2 Flower Roll out the bright yellow sugarpaste to a thickness of ⅛in (2–3mm) on a surface dusted with icing sugar and cut one large flower shape with your cutter. Stick it in the centre of the cake with a little brushed-on water.

3 Second flower Repeat and cut out a second sunflower or daisy shape, position this on top so that the second layer of petals fill the gaps between the first ones.

4 Head Squash the ball of pale yellow sugarpaste until it is 1⅕in (30mm) across, and make two holes at the top ready for the ears.

5 Ears Squash each of the two balls for the ears flat, and pinch one side to make a point.

6 Add ears Insert these points into the holes in the head; push the pointed end of the modelling tool into the centre of each ear to secure.

7 Nose Make a nice big hole in the centre of the face ready for the nose to be added. Form the round ball for the nose into a teardrop shape and insert the pointed end into the hole.

8 Pointy nose When the nose is in place, use the pointed end of your modelling tool to gently drag three points outwards to create a more triangular shaped nose.

9 Facial features Paint a little mouth under the nose; dilute the black paste colour first with water if it is too thick to paint with. Mark the eyes (see 'How to mark eyes', page 143) with black paste colour and a cocktail stick (or toothpick). Tiny dots for eyebrows can be added too.

10 Add head Add the head to the centre of your cupcake. Stick in place with a little water or royal icing to secure.

This little hippo is sure to be a hit! If your cake is chocolate,
why not put him in brown mud icing instead of blue water?
You could also paint your spaghetti reeds with green food colouring.

Wallowing hippo

Materials

Grey sugarpaste (see pages 138–39)

Blue royal icing or filling cream (see pages 148–49)

No. 9 modelling tool

Black paste food colour

Cocktail stick or toothpick

Several pieces of uncooked spaghetti

Part	Template	Colour
Bottom	E	Grey
Tail	G	Grey
Head	D	Grey
Ears	G (divide into 2)	Grey

See templates for sizes on page 132

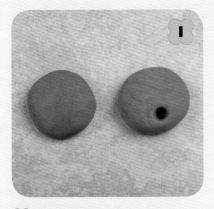

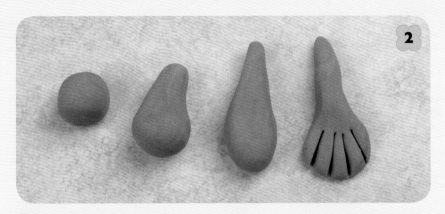

1 Bottom Slightly flatten the ball of grey sugarpaste for the bottom, then make a deep hole in it with the pointed end of your modelling tool.

2 Tail Form the ball for the tail into a teardrop shape, elongate then flatten the larger end and mark with four or five little lines using the back of a knife.

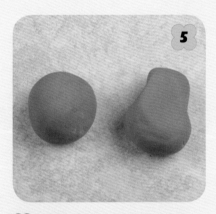

3 Add tail Firmly push the pointed end of the tail into the deep hole; bend the flat end down slightly.

4 Water Cover the top of the cake with a generous quantity of turquoise blue royal icing or filling cream (see page 142). Spike it up into points and place the hippo's bottom into it.

5 Head Form the pear-shaped head from a ball of grey sugarpaste. Flatten the top of the head to make it thinner than the fat nose end.

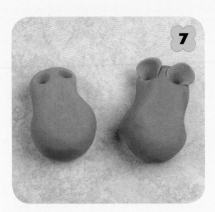

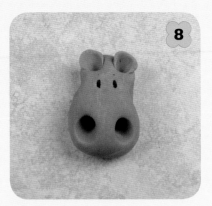

6 **Ears** Divide the ball for the ears into two, then form each piece into a round ball, flatten, and pinch one side to make each ear.

7 **Attach ears** Make two deep holes at the very top of the hippo's head with the pointed end of the modelling tool, and then firmly push each ear into place.

8 **Nostrils and eyes** At the opposite end of his head make two huge holes for his nostrils; twist the tool as you push it in to make the holes bigger. Mark the eyes (see 'how to mark eyes', page 143) with black paste colour using a cocktail stick (or toothpick) and tiny dots for the eyebrows too.

9 **Add head** Place the head into the top of the icing and position it so that it is slightly hanging over the side.

10 **Reeds** Gently spray the blue water with pearl lustre spray and push in some short pieces of raw spaghetti for reeds.

This bright-eyed tiger is peeping out of the jungle – waiting to pounce!
Lion (page 59) and snake (page 47) cakes would complement this
tiger to create a real jungle theme.

Tiger

Materials

Green, orange, white and black sugarpaste (see pages 138–39)

Lime green royal icing (see page 149)

No. 9 modelling tool

Black paste food colour

Cocktail stick or toothpick

No. 43 small star piping tube and piping bags (see page 144)

Green food colour (optional)

Paintbrush

Icing sugar

Part	Template	Colour
Head	D	Orange
Nose	E	White
Nose tip	H	Black
Tail	F	Orange
Ears	G (divide in two)	Orange

See templates for sizes on page 132

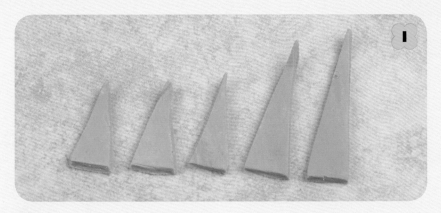

1 **Grass** Cut some pieces of grass from your green sugarpaste (see templates on page 151) rolled out on a work surface dusted with icing sugar. They want to be between 1–1½in (25–40mm) long. Allow to dry.

2 **Head** Form the three balls of sugarpaste, ready to make the tiger's head. Shape the largest orange one into an oval shape.

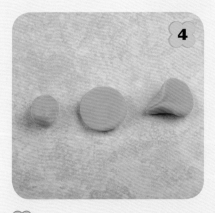

3 **Nose** Join the white ball of icing to the orange one, using a little brushed-on water to stick if necessary. Make a hole in the white piece and stick in the black nose. Make two more holes at the top of the head ready for the ears.

4 **Ears** Form the two balls for the ears, squash each one and pinch one side of it to form a little ear, then push one into each large hole.

5 **Eyes and stripes** Mark the eyes (see 'How to mark eyes', page 143) and tiny dots for eyebrows too. Dilute a little black paste colour with a drop of water and paint on the tiger stripes with a fine paintbrush.

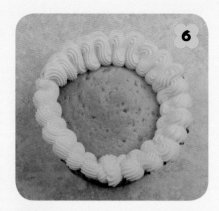

6 Wavy line Place a star tube in the piping bag and half fill with lime green royal icing. Pipe a wavy line all around the edge of your cake.

7 Seal cupcake Continue piping the green wavy lines until all your cupcake is covered with icing; this will seal the cake and keep it fresh.

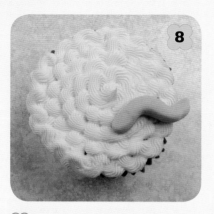

8 Tail Shape the ball for the tail into a sausage 1in (25mm). Place this on top of the lime green royal icing, slightly overhanging the cake edge.

9 Add head Place the head on to the cake, covering the end of the tail. Be careful not to smudge the black stripes when you pick it up.

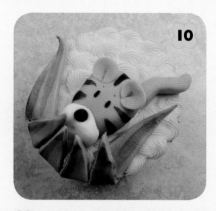

10 Attach grass Finally, add the spiky grass pieces, piping extra lime green royal icing to hold them in place. If you wish, paint a little green colour on to the spikes to give a streaky effect.

Pigs always make popular and fun little characters. If your party has a farmyard theme, then this could be perfect as your cupcake design.

Pig in mud

Materials

Pale pink, black and white sugarpaste (see pages 138–39)

Chocolate brown royal icing or filling cream (see page 148–49)

Green royal icing (see page 149)

No. 9 modelling tool

Small piping bag (see pages 144–45)

Round cutters

Paintbrush

Part	Template	Colour
Tail	F	Pale pink
Ears	2 x F	Pale pink
White eye	H	White
Black eye	J	Black

See templates for sizes on page 132

1 Cover cupcake Spread the top of your cupcake generously with chocolate coloured royal icing or filling cream (see page 142), then make a slightly swirly pattern in the top of it.

2 Tail Form the tail into a tapered sausage shape 1in (25mm) long, and curl it around, then place at the top of the cupcake.

3 Body Roll out a piece of pink sugarpaste to a thickness of ⅛in (4mm) and cut a disc 2in (50mm) in diameter. Place on top of your cupcake covering the end of the tail.

4 Face Cut another disc of pink sugarpaste 1⅛in (30mm) wide and place this at the bottom of the face sticking with a little brushed-on water.

5 Nose Using the pointed end of the modelling tool, make two very deep holes, pushing all the way down to the chocolate colour under the pink.

6 Eyes Form two white oval shapes from the two balls of white sugarpaste for the white eyes, and stick them above the nose with a little brushed-on water. Place a black ball on the lower part of the white to complete each eye.

7 **Ears** To make the ears, squash each of the balls of pink sugarpaste flat and then pinch one side together.

8 **Attach ears** Stick the ears to the top of the pig's head. The two points need to be a lot higher than the top of the head.

9 **Bend ears** Bend the pointed top of each ear firmly downwards to shape the ears; the pig's face is now completed.

10 **Grass** Place a small amount of green royal icing into a small piping bag and pipe some spikes of green grass under the pig's face (see page 145).

This happy clown will be everybody's favourite and an essential character for any children's party. Why not give him some more bright ruffles around his neck for an extra colourful effect?

Clown

Materials

White, red, orange and green sugarpaste (see pages 138–39)

No. 9 modelling tool

Garrett frill cutter

Round cutters

Small star cutter

Black paste food colour

Cocktail stick or toothpick

Paintbrush

Icing sugar

Part	Template	Colour
Head	B	White
Nose	G	Red

See templates for sizes on page 132

1 Head and nose Squash the ball for the head flat onto your work surface. Form the red nose into a pointy teardrop shape. Make a big hole in the centre of the face with the pointed end of your modelling tool, and insert the nose.

2 Hat and stars Prepare the hat and star shapes. Roll out orange and red sugarpaste to a thickness of ⅛in (2–3mm) and cut the triangular hat shape (see template on page 151). Cut out lots of orange stars too, three for each clown you are making.

3 Add head and ears Stick the clown's head on the blue covered cupcake and gently mark two rounded impressions for the ears, using the round end of the modelling tool. Stick two stars above the ears with a little brushed-on water.

4 Eyes Mark two long friendly eyes (see 'How to mark eyes', page 143) on the clown's face with black paste colour and a cocktail stick (or toothpick).

5 Cut the collar Roll out a piece of white or coloured sugarpaste on a surface dusted with icing sugar to a thickness of ⅛in (2–3mm), and cut out a circle with a garrett frill cutter.

6 Collar From this circle you will get four collars for your clowns. Mark and cut four pieces. These can be made in any colour and two or three can also be used on the same clown.

7 **Frills** Using a modelling tool, follow the instructions on page 147 and frill along the outside of your piece of sugarpaste.

8 **Attach frills** Using a little water or royal icing, stick the frill or frills below the clown's face. If you are sticking on more than one, overlap them so you can see the colour underneath.

9 **Add hat** Stick the little red hat to the blue surface of the cake using some brushed-on water to secure it.

10 **Add star and smile** Finally, stick on the last orange star on top of the clown's hat and paint on a lovely big smile with black paste colour and a paintbrush.

The top of a slightly domed muffin is perfect for this pretty
little fish bowl design. Make different shapes and colours
of fish on all your cupcakes.

Fish bowl

Materials

White, orange and grey sugarpaste (see pages 138–39)

Green royal icing (see page 149)

No. 9 modelling tool

Piping bags (see pages 144–45)

Black paste food colour

Cocktail stick or toothpick

Pearl lustre spray

Yellow and blue food colour

Paintbrushes

Icing sugar

Part	Template	Colour
Fish body	Small E	Orange
Rim of bowl	F	White

See templates for sizes on page 132

1 **Sand** Cover the top of the slightly domed cupcake in white sugarpaste (see page 142), paint an uneven strip of yellow along the base. Using a piece of spaghetti, make lots of indents in it to create a sandy effect.

2 **Water** Paint a streaky water effect above the sand with a large paintbrush, dilute your food colour with water as you don't want the water too dark.

3 **Rim of bowl** Form a sausage from the ball of white sugarpaste, taper the ends and wrap it around the top of the goldfish bowl, sticking it with a little brushed-on water.

4 **Fish** Form the piece of orange sugarpaste into a teardrop shape, then flatten it and pinch a point at the end.

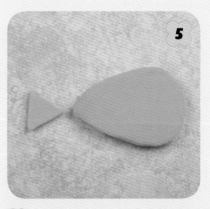

5 **Fish tail** On a surface dusted with icing sugar, roll out a little piece of orange sugarpaste and cut out the little triangular tails (see template, page 151).

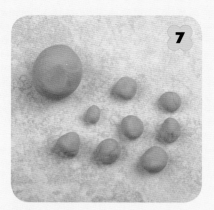

6 **Fins** Mark the tail with a knife blade to make lines along it. Also mark the fishes' fins on each side of its body by pressing in a knife blade – make them deep but do not cut through. Mark the eyes (see 'How to mark eyes', page 143) with black paste colour and a cocktail stick (or toothpick). Add a little line for the mouth.

7 **Pebbles** Make pebbles, all different sizes from the grey sugarpaste. They look nice marbled so don't mix the grey colour in completely.

8 **Add pebbles** Using a little brushed-on water, stick the tiny pebbles along the edge of the yellow at the top of the sand, leave a gap in the centre instead of making a straight line.

9 **Attach fish** Pop the little fish on to the front of the fish tank, sticking with a little brushed-on water. If you make your fish small you will be able to fit more than one in the bowl.

10 **Pond plants** Half fill a small piping bag with green royal icing. Cut a straight hole off the end and pipe wiggly lines both sides of the bowl. Spray all over with pearl lustre spray.

Everyone loves dolphins and this little one leaping out of the water will make someone's birthday very special. You can make your dolphin's body the day before you need it.

Dolphin

Materials

Grey and blue sugarpaste (see pages 138–39)

Turquoise and white royal icing (see page 149)

Black paste food colour

Cocktail stick or toothpick

Pearl lustre spray

Fine paintbrush

Palette knife

Part	Template	Colour
Body	D	Grey
Tail	F	Grey

See templates for sizes on page 132

 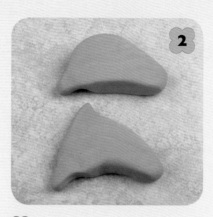 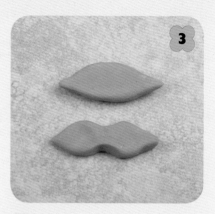

1 Body From the ball of grey sugarpaste, form a pear shape ready to create the dolphin's body, then slightly flatten it.

2 Nose and dorsal fin Curve one side downwards and pinch a little nose at the fatter end, stretch and pull the other end and curve it. Pull and pinch a fin on top of the body.

3 Tail fins Shape the tail into an oval and pinch both ends to a point, then squash it in the middle.

4 Tail fins Pinch it together at the centre to create a tail shape. Now pinch both ends of the tail fins to make nice points.

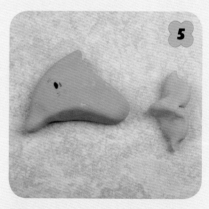

5 Eyes Mark a little eye on each side of the dolphin's face (see 'How to mark eyes', page 143) with black paste colour and a cocktail stick (or toothpick). Paint a few faint black lines around the eye too.

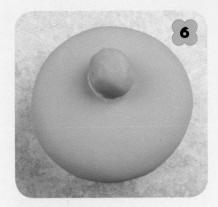

6 Sea Cover the cupcake with blue sugarpaste, then place a ball of blue sugarpaste on top to hold the dolphin up out of the waves.

7 Making waves Cover the ball and the top of the sugarpaste with turquoise royal icing using a knife to pull it into nice high points.

8 Finishing waves Add some white royal icing to the tops of the waves and blend it in with the blue icing using a palette knife to swirl it all together.

9 Attach tail fins Push the little tail fins into the edge of the cupcake making sure they are held securely in the royal icing sea.

10 Attach body Add the dolphin's body, resting it over the ball of blue so it looks like it is jumping out of the waves. Spray some pearl lustre spray on to the water to give the 'sea' a lovely shimmer.

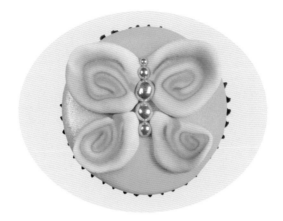

This is a lovely technique to learn and great fun to do with children.
They love discovering what pattern has been made inside,
and experimenting with all different colours.

Butterfly

Materials

Dark pink, purple, white and dark blue sugarpaste
  (see pages 138–39)
Apricot purée (see page 149)
Pearl lustre spray
Silver dragées (balls) in various sizes
Icing sugar

1 Roll sugarpaste Roll out the four pieces of sugarpaste and place them on top of each other.

2 Join together Roll over them; this will squash and join them together. Roll one end over tightly.

3 Roll tightly Continue to roll tightly until you reach the end of the icing, and then tuck the end underneath.

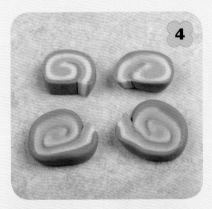

4 Wings Cut little slices with a sharp knife; for small wings cut thin slices and thick slices for larger wings.

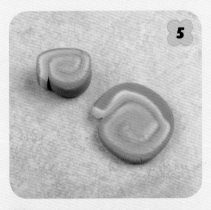

5 Large wings Place them on your work surface and roll over the top surface if you want them to be larger.

6 Cover cupcake Cover the cupcake with a disc of sugarpaste (see page 142). Start to stick the wings to the top of the cupcake with a little brushed-on water or apricot purée.

7 Add remaining wings Add the last two wings, and stick in place; make sure the patterns are mirror images.

8 Body While your butterfly is still soft, push in silver dragées that make up the body. Press them in well so they stay in place.

9 Decorate cupcake Spray your cupcake all over with pearl lustre spray to soften the colours and give it a shimmery effect.

10 Alternate layers This butterfly has been made with the same colours as the previous one but layered in a different order.

This jaunty little sailing boat could be made in many
different bright colours, but remember to make the sails
a day in advance to allow them to dry completely.

Sailing boat

Materials

Red, turquoise and blue sugarpaste (see pages 138–39)

Pastillage (see page 150)

White and turquoise royal icing (see page 149)

No. 9 modelling tool

Piping bags (see pages 144–45)

No. 1 piping tube

Pearl lustre spray

Red food colouring

Paintbrush or an icing pen

Palette knife

Disco white hologram edible glitter

Icing sugar

Note:

The sails are made from pastillage in advance (see step 4).

1 Boat Cut a little boat shape 1½in (35mm) long from a block of red sugarpaste.

2 Mark lines Soften the edges of the boat by rubbing with your palms gently and mark two lines all around the sides with a knife.

3 Mark holes Push in three holes along each side of the boat with the pointed end of a modelling tool.

4 Sails Cut the sails in advance from pastillage rolled out to a thickness of ½in (2mm), using the templates on page 151. Allow them to dry on a work surface dusted with icing sugar.

5 Add large sail When they are dry (in 24 hours), push the largest sail into the boat firmly enough for it to stay in place.

6 Add second sail Now add the second smaller sail so that it neatly joins the first one.

7 Dividing dots Half fill a small piping bag with a No. I piping tube with royal icing and pipe a row of little dots between the two sails.

8 Decorate sails You can write the age of a child or adult on a sail with a fine paintbrush or an icing pen.

9 Waves Cover the cupcake with a disc of turquoise blue sugarpaste and spread a little blue royal icing in the middle; peak it up using the side of a palette knife. Spray the surface of the icing all over with pearl lustre spray.

10 Add boat Position the boat in the waves and sprinkle on some edible glitter to make the sea look sparkly!

This graceful swan is trickier than some of the other designs but worth it for the end result. Put two smaller swans together for an engagement or anniversary cake.

Swan

Materials

White and blue sugarpaste (see pages 138–39)

Pastillage (see page 150)

White royal icing (see page 149)

Piping bag (see pages 144–45)

Pearl lustre spray

Paintbrush

Clear piping gel

Black paste food colour

Orange food colour

Part	Template	Colour
Body	C – sugarpaste and F – pastillage mixed together	White
Wings	2 x F	White

See templates for sizes on page 132

Notes:

For the body you need to mix a little pastillage with the white sugarpaste so that the neck will support itself without breaking or drooping. Blend the two balls together (see recipe for pastillage, page 150).

The body should be left for 24 hours before you paint on the details of the beak.

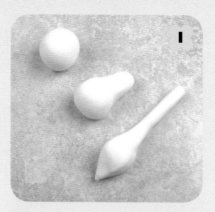

1 Body Form the body firstly into a pear shape, then elongate the narrower end until it is 2in (50mm) long. Pinch a point at the fat end for the tail.

2 Neck Start to bend the swan's neck up from a third of the way in from the tail point. If you bend it further along it will flop down.

3 Beak When the neck is bent back and forward again in a curve, pinch in a long thin beak with your thumb and index finger. Roll the neck of the swan between your fingers gently to thin it slightly and make the head look fatter.

4 Head Now curve the head of the swan around so that she looks like she is resting it on the front of her body. Be careful not to bend the beak, as it needs to remain straight.

5 Let dry Leave her to dry in this position while you make her little wings.

6 Mould wings Mould the wings each into a teardrop shape, slightly bend the point upwards, then flatten and mark on the feathered effect with a knife.

7 Add wings The wings can be stuck to the side of the swan with royal icing. Be sure to mark the ruffled feather effect on the correct side.

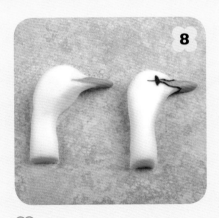

8 Face Paint the orange onto the swan's face first as on the sample pieces above. Allow it to dry and then with a fine paintbrush, paint the thin black line and the long eyes.

9 Water Roll out and cut a slightly larger circle than the top of the case. When you place your icing on, it should slope up at the edges to make a well in the centre. Fill the well with clear piping gel for the water.

10 Grass Place the finished swan in the centre of the pond. Half fill a small piping bag with white royal icing and cut the end of the paper to pipe grass (see page 145). Pipe all around the edges of the pond then spray all over with pearl lustre spray.

Cover your cupcake in delightful mini cupcakes – make them single or multi-layered – what a lovely teatime treat! If you don't have a cupcake mould you could finish the top with a chocolate or a coloured sweet.

Mini cupcakes

Materials

Mini cupcake mould
Cornflour
Pastillage (see page 150)
White sugarpaste (see pages 138–39)
White and red royal icing (see page 149)
Piping bags (see pages 144–45)

No. 42 small star tube and No. 1 piping tube
Paintbrushes
Gold dragées (balls)
Pink, red and gold yellow food colours
White satin shimmer
Painting solution (or white alcohol)

1 Mini cupcakes Take a small ball of the sugarpaste/pastillage mixture, dust its surface lightly with cornflour, and press it firmly into the mould. Cut back neatly level with the edge of the mould and remove.

2 Paint cupcakes Make lots of little cupcakes, allow to dry for 24 hours and then paint with food colour diluted with painting solution. To create a shimmery paint effect, mix in white satin shimmer.

3 Cover cupcakes Use a slightly domed cake for this design (see page 141). Cover the cupcakes with a disc of white sugarpaste (see page 142). Using a large brush, paint white satin shimmer onto the top.

4 Double up If you wish to double up the cupcakes, stick the smaller one on top while the lower one is still soft, using a little royal icing piped underneath to hold in place.

5 Stars This design has been finished with piped royal icing around the edge of the cupcake (see 'Piping royal icing with a star tube', page 146).

6 **Small dots** Place a small amount of red royal icing in a small bag with a No. 1 piping tube and pipe little dots all over the pink surface. Stick your mini cupcake on top with a little white royal icing to hold in place.

7 **Decorating ideas** Pipe a wavy line all around the outer edge of this pale gold cupcake. While the royal icing is still soft, press in gold dragées. Start to pipe red dots all over the surface (see step 6).

8 **Stars** Stick another small cupcake on top and pipe stars all around its outer edge (see step 5). Pipe a large swirl of royal icing on top and gently push in one of the mini cupcakes.

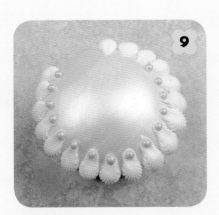

9 **Shells** Pipe royal icing shells with your star tube pointing upwards, practise this first on your work surface, as it is a little tricky to get them all the same size (see 'Piping royal icing with a star tube', page 146).

10 **Finish the design** Add the top tier and repeat the shells all around its top edge too. Pipe stars around the bottom of the case and add some gold dragées. Complete the design with a mini cupcake on top.

Make these little cupcakes for any occasion. You could always pop a candle in the centre of each birthday cake too and make the mats in different colours to match your cake cases.

Picnic time

Materials

White, red, chocolate and green sugarpaste
   (see pages 138–39)
White and red royal icing (see page 149)
Quilting tool
Piping bags (see pages 144–45)
Nos. 1 and 2 piping tubes

For the chocolate cake:

Number of balls	Template	Colour
3	D	Chocolate
2	E	White

See templates for sizes on page 132

1 Picnic mat Roll out and cut little squares of white sugarpaste 2in (50mm) square and ⅛in (2–3mm) thick. Place three very thin sausages of red sugarpaste across the square and roll over it with a small rolling pin to stick them in place.

2 Decorate mat Place two more thin red sausages across the square in the opposite direction and roll over once again to stick in place.

3 Trim mat Cut neatly down each side of the picnic mat to trim away any uneven edges.

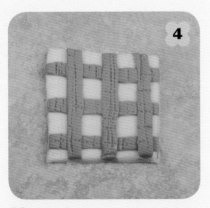

4 Add texture Using a quilting tool, run it back and forth across the mat to give it some texture; repeat in the other direction too.

5 Cover cupcake Cover the top of the cupcake in a round disc of green sugarpaste and stick your picnic mat on top of it.

6 Chocolate cake To make the chocolate cake, form three round balls of chocolate sugarpaste and two smaller ones in white sugarpaste.

7 Layer the cake Start to layer the balls by squashing them, then placing them on top of each other alternately. When they are all in place flatten the cake top slightly.

8 Add cake Pop the birthday cake on top of the picnic mat and, using a knife, make three lines across the top making six sections of cake.

9 Pipe balls Half fill a small piping bag with a No. 2 tube with white royal icing and pipe a ball in each section of the cake. Pipe a slightly larger ball in the centre too. Allow these balls to dry for an hour before you move to step 10.

10 Cherry Place a small amount of red royal icing in a piping bag with a No. 1 tube and pipe a cherry on top of the white balls to complete the cake.

This beehive cake is a firm favourite and there is lots of icing on it so children will love it. You could also pop some sweets into the hollow beehive as a surprise!

Beehive

Materials

Yellow, white and green sugarpaste (see pages 138–39)

Pastillage (see page 150)

Green and white royal icing (see page 149)

Piping bag (see pages 144–45)

Black paste food colour

No. 24 flower wires

Paintbrush

Icing sugar

Part	Template	Colour
Bee	G	Yellow
Wings	2 x 1	White
First ring	B	White
Second ring	C	White
Third ring	D	White
Fourth ring	E	White
Fifth section	F	White
Sixth section	G	White

See templates for sizes on page 132

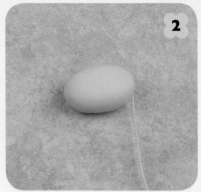

Tip

If you don't want to use wires in your cakes just stick the little bees to the outside of your beehive instead of putting wires into them.

1 Body Mix a little pastillage with the yellow sugarpaste to allow the bee's body to set hard around the flower wire. Form the yellow sugarpaste/pastillage mix into a tiny oval shape.

2 Add wire Bend around ⅛in (2–3mm) of wire over the top to form a right angle. Brush a little water or sugar glue on to the end and push it into the bee's body.

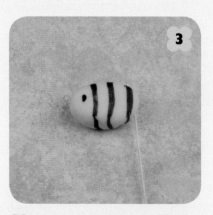

3 Stripes and eyes Allow to dry for several hours or overnight, and then paint the thin black stripes on both sides of the body. Paint on the little eyes.

4 Wings Make some little balls of pastillage and squash flat on to a little icing sugar, for the bee's wings then dry.

5 Attach wings When the wings are dry, brush off any excess icing sugar and stick one each side of the bee's body with a little piped blob of white royal icing.

6 Cover cupcake Cover the top of the cupcake with a bright green disc of sugarpaste. Stick it to the top with either apricot purée or filling cream.

7 First ring From the ball of white sugarpaste, form a sausage 5in (130mm) long, bend it into a circle, and stick to the top of the cake.

8 Second ring Form a sausage from the ball of white sugarpaste, roll around, and place on top of the first ring. Repeat again for the third ring.

9 Fourth ring One more ring needs to go on top and the last two sections are just slightly squashed balls of white sugarpaste.

10 Add bees and grass Add three little bees to the beehive by pushing the wires into the icing. Complete with a few little blades of grass piped at the base (see page 145).

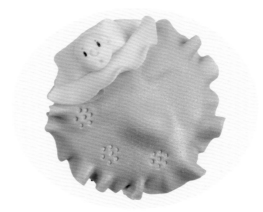

This is a delightful design, not only suitable for a christening but pop little animals in the bed for a children's birthday cake idea – the dog, hippo or pig would look great in here.

New baby

Materials

White, pale blue and pale peach sugarpaste
  (see pages 138–39)
No. 9 modelling tool
Round cutters
Black paste food colour
Cocktail stick or toothpick
Pearl lustre spray
Piece of uncooked spaghetti
Icing sugar

Part	Template	Colour
Pillow	E	White
Body	G	White
Head	Small E	Pale peach
Nose	J	Pale peach

See templates for sizes on page 132

1 **Pillow** Form the ball of white sugarpaste for the pillow into a sausage shape 2in (50mm) long. Cut off the ends and press your little finger in the centre to create a dent for the head.

2 **Add pillow and body** Place the pillow at the very top of the bed – half on and half off the cake. Stick with a little brushed-on water. Add the baby's body to the centre.

3 **Frill** Cut a strip of white sugarpaste 2in (50mm) long, frill all the way along one long edge (see 'How to frill sugarpaste', page 147).

4 **Attach frill** Place this little strip over the pillow with the frill at the top of the bed almost completely covering the pillow.

5 **Blanket** Roll out a circle of pale blue sugarpaste, 3in (75mm) in diameter. Cut a section off the top with a knife, leaving a straight line.

6 **Frill blanket** Frill this piece of sugarpaste all the way around the edge (see 'How to frill sugarpaste', page 147). Use plenty of icing sugar underneath to stop it from sticking to your work surface.

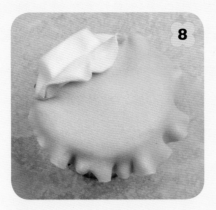

7 Add blanket Place it on top of your cake showing ⅖in (10mm) of white frill at the top. Stick it in place with a little brushed-on water, then spray all over with pearl lustre spray.

8 Turn blanket down Turn down the white frill so that it shows as a frilly under blanket and exposing all of the pillow ready for the baby's head.

9 Head Make the baby's head from the ball of pale peach sugarpaste. Mark the ears on each side of the head with the pointed end of a modelling tool. Insert a teardrop-shaped nose into a hole in the centre of the face and mark the eyes (see 'How to mark eyes', page 143). Make a little mouth hole under the nose. Place the head on the pillow.

10 Flowers Finally, impress little flower shapes all over the blue bedspread with the end of a piece of spaghetti.

This cake could be suitable for any young child's party or even for a christening or new baby celebration. The teddies and blankets could be made in many different colours.

Teddy bear

Materials

Red, 'teddy bear' brown, chocolate brown and yellow
   sugarpaste (see pages 138–39)
No. 9 modelling tool
Quilting tool
Black paste food colour
Cocktail stick or toothpick
Paintbrush
Piece of uncooked spaghetti

Part	Template	Colour
Body	D	Teddy bear brown
Feet	2 × small G	Teddy bear brown
Arms	2 × G	Teddy bear brown
Head	Large E	Teddy bear brown
Nose	Large H	Teddy bear brown
Nose tip	I	Chocolate brown
Ears	2 × H	Teddy bear brown
Blanket	Large D	Yellow

See templates for sizes on page 132

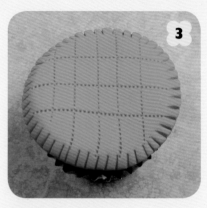

1 Cover cupcake Roll out and cut out a disc the same size as the top of your cupcake in red sugarpaste (see page 142). Mark little lines around the outside edge with a sharp knife.

2 Stitches When all the lines have been marked around the outside of the disc, use the quilting tool to run little stitched lines across the cake in one direction.

3 Add texture Using the quilting tool, make more lines across the first ones to create a textured look to the top of the cake.

4 Body and feet Start to form the teddy bear. Shape the body into a cone and then push on two round balls for the feet. If necessary, a little water can be brushed on to stick them down.

5 Arm Each arm is a long cone shape. Stick one to each side of the body with the point at the top. Push in a piece of spaghetti to support the head, break it off with a little bit showing.

6 Head and nose Form the head. Press on the small round nose. Make the nose tip into a ball shape and press on to the top of the nose; a little brushed-on water can help secure it.

7 Ears Shape each ear. Flatten the round ball, pinch one side, make two holes in the top of the head, and push in the points. Secure in place by pushing the pointed end of your modelling tool into the centre of each ear. Place the head onto the spaghetti.

8 Eyes and tummy button
Mark the eyes (see 'How to mark eyes', page 143) with black paste colour and a cocktail stick (or toothpick). Mark two tiny dots for eyebrows, then make the mouth hole with a modelling tool and the tummy button with the tip of a cocktail stick.

9 Blanket From a round ball of yellow sugarpaste, squash the yellow blanket until it is quite thin, then fold and crumple it slightly.

10 Add blanket and teddy
Stick the blanket to the cake with brushed-on water, and pop the teddy bear on top. Why not make a little duck too? (See Duck pond, page 10.)

These are perfect for a wedding. Make single large muffins or make a little tiered wedding cake with three different sizes on top of each other. The colour of the cases could coordinate with the theme of the wedding.

Wedding cupcakes

Materials
3 sizes of cupcakes in gold cases with flat tops (see page 141)

White sugarpaste (see pages 138–39)

Pastillage (see page 150)

White royal icing (see page 149)

No. 9 modelling tool

Piping bags (see pages 144–45)

Round cutters

Pearl lustre spray

Icing sugar

Part	Template
Roses: centre	E
All petals	F

See templates for sizes on page 132

Use a fifth pastillage and four-fifths sugarpaste to make the roses.

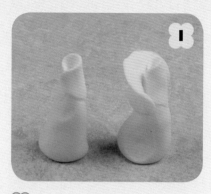

1 Rose centre and petals
Form a very pointy cone from the sugarpaste/pastillage mix, and allow to dry for at least an hour. Squash the petal very thinly on one edge and wrap around the top of the point. Add another directly over the join of the previous petal but don't stick down the last edge.

2 Third petal Form the third petal and tuck it under the edge of the previous petal, wrap it around but don't stick down the edge of it, as the last petal always tucks under the previous one. If the petals don't stick by themselves, use a little brushed-on water to secure.

3 Attach third petal Add the third petal in this layer, this time you can stick down the final edge as this layer is complete. If you wish to add another layer to make the rose larger, the next layer will have five petals.

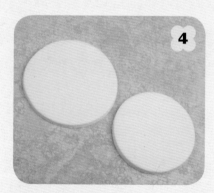

4 Cut out circles Roll out a piece of white sugarpaste on a surface lightly dusted with icing sugar. Cut a disc ⅘in (20mm) larger than the top of your cupcake. Cut another disc ⅖in (10mm) smaller than the first.

5 Frill Start to frill (see 'How to frill sugarpaste', page 147) around the disc of icing. Always have lots of icing sugar on the work surface to prevent the frill from sticking. Frill both circles all the way around.

6 Attach large frill Stick your largest frill on top of your cupcake with either a little filling cream or apricot purée. Make sure it is stuck well so it seals all the sponge mixture below.

7 Add small circle Stick the smaller disc in the centre of the first one and use the pointed end of your modelling tool to tweak up the edges of the frills so that it looks really flouncy.

8 Leaves Press a dip in the centre of your cake for the rose to sit in. Break off the back of the rose and stick it in the middle of the cupcake. Pipe leaves with white royal icing all around the flower (see page 145) and spray your cake with pearl lustre spray. This completes the top tier.

9 More tiers For the three-tier cupcake, you need to start with three different sizes of cupcake; if they aren't flat on top place a disc of icing in each one to make them level.

10 Finish the design
Two layers of frill go on each cake, Layer each cake on top of the one below while the surface is still soft, and it will stick better. Finish with a little rose on top, spray with pearl lustre spray and use edible glitter for a final effect.

Tip
If you are in a hurry, you can buy a variety of ready-made sugar flowers to decorate the top.

This floral design would work with or without the little ladybird and could be done in many colours. You could also make some flowers with little bees on them for a variation.

Ladybird

Materials

Purple, yellow, red and black sugarpaste (see pages 138–39)

No. 9 modelling tool

Black paste food colour

Cocktail stick or toothpick

Round cutters

Icing sugar

Part	Template	Colour
Body	G	Red
Head	H (makes 2)	Black
Flower centre	F	Yellow

See templates for sizes on page 132

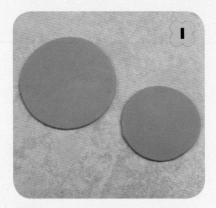

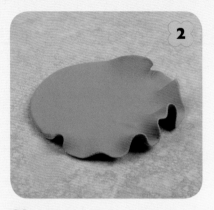

1 **Cut out circles** Roll out the purple sugarpaste on a work surface dusted with icing sugar. Cut two circles ⅛in (3–4mm) thick. One circle needs to be the size of the cupcake top and the other one ⅕in (20mm) smaller.

2 **Frill circles** Frill (see 'How to frill sugarpaste', page 147) the circles all the way around using a modelling tool.

3 **Add frill** Using filling cream or a little brushed on apricot purée, stick the frill to the top of the cupcake.

4 **Flower centre** Arrange the second smaller frill on top and with a knife, then mark some lines pointed into the centre, all the way round. Squash a ball of yellow sugarpaste on to the centre of the flower.

5 **Mark holes** Using the pointed end of a modelling tool, mark little holes all the way around the outside of the circle in the middle.

6 Add holes to centre Now, make little holes all over the centre of it, once again using the pointed end of the modelling tool.

7 Body and head Form your little red ball for the ladybird's body into an oval shape. Also form the black ball into an oval, squash it and cut in half to make two heads.

8 Add head Using a little water to secure, stick the black head on to the ladybird's body. Mark a line right down the ladybird's back with a knife.

9 Spots and eyes Dip a cocktail stick (or toothpick) into the black paste colour and push it into the ladybird's red body to make the spots, also mark two eyes using the pointed end of the modelling tool.

10 Add ladybird Place the ladybird on to the lovely ~~~~ to complete your design

These flower cutters are so versatile that many different designs can be created with a little bit of imagination and using a variety of colours. These pretty cakes are perfect for a wedding or birthday celebration.

Funky flowers

Materials

White, chocolate, pink and blue sugarpaste (see pages 138–39)

Pastillage, optional (see page 150)

White, pink and light blue royal icing (see page 149)

Large and small funky flower cutters

Piping bags (see pages 144–45)

No. 1 piping tube

Pearl lustre spray

Paintbrushes

White satin shimmer

Flat make-up sponge

Brown food colour

...he little
purple flower
on

1 Cover cupcake For this design you need a cupcake with a domed top (see page 141). Cover the cupcake with a circle of mid-blue sugarpaste, smooth it gently with your hands to neatly join the case all the way round (see page 142).

2 Add a sheen Dip a flat round make-up sponge into white satin shimmer and polish it all over your cupcakes to give a beautiful sheen.

3 Funky flower cutters There are four different sizes of funky flower cutters that can be used together in many ways. Layering is particularly effective.

4 Large flower Roll out the white sugarpaste or sugarpaste/ pastillage mix to a thinness of ⅛in (2–3mm). Cut the largest shape of funky flower and stick it on top of the cake with a little water.

5 Medium flower Double up the flowers by cutting the next size down and sticking it to the centre of the previous flower. Press your finger into the centre to create a small dip.

6 Small flower The smallest cutter has been used here to cut a shape from the largest funky flower. Keep the middle flower you have removed as you can use it on another cake for layering.

7 Pipe dots Half fill a piping bag and No. 1 tube with white royal icing. Pipe a circle of dots in the centre of the flower, then pipe dots randomly all around the rest of the blue surface. Finally, pipe dots all around the edge. To finish, spray with pearl lustre spray.

8 White funky flowers This cake has been layered with three funky flowers, decreasing in size, but all in white. Pipe pink royal icing from a No. 1 tube in a flower pattern in the centre and pink dots all the way around the outer edge. Spray all over with pearl lustre spray.

9 Two funky flowers The largest flower is cut from white sugarpaste, then the next size down in chocolate colour. Squash a little pink ball into the centre and complete with piped pink dots on top, and pale blue piping around the edges.

10 Three layers Before you do the piping in step 9, add a small white flower to the centre to give it three layers, and complete with pink piped dots and painted chocolate lines.

Techniques

How to make your cupcakes crafty

Sugarpaste templates

If you are a beginner, practise making a duck before you make one of the more complicated models. Always use the templates below for all your animals and people, as this will save you having to guess the size of each body part.

All the models in this book have been made with bought sugarpaste/rolled fondant icing. I have used Regalice throughout. If you use a different brand, ensure that it isn't too sticky or too elastic in texture.

Method

Each time you create a part of your model, roll it into a smooth ball in the palm of your hands. The warmth of your hands will soften the paste and remove any lines or cracks from its surface. Now match the ball to the correct size ball on the chart.

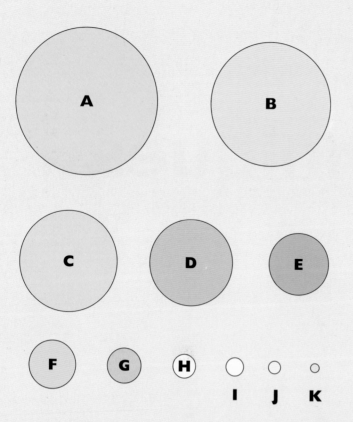

Tip

If your instructions say to use a 'Small A' size, form a ball that fits well inside the outline. Alternatively a 'Large B' would cover the outer rim of the circle.

Equipment for decorating

Large sunflower cutter

Small blossom cutter

Small star cutter

Garrett frill cutter

Rolling pin

Set of round cutters

Small and large funky flower cutters (AP)

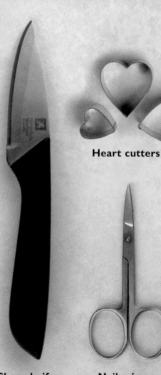

Heart cutters

Sharp knife

Nail scissors

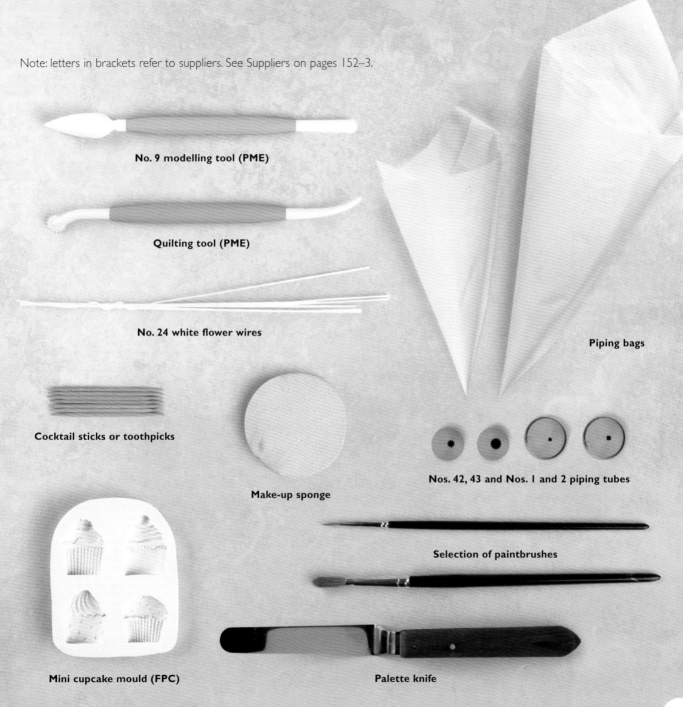

Note: letters in brackets refer to suppliers. See Suppliers on pages 152–3.

No. 9 modelling tool (PME)

Quilting tool (PME)

No. 24 white flower wires

Piping bags

Cocktail sticks or toothpicks

Make-up sponge

Nos. 42, 43 and Nos. 1 and 2 piping tubes

Selection of paintbrushes

Mini cupcake mould (FPC)

Palette knife

Ingredients for decorating

Filling cream

Royal icing

Apricot purée

Icing sugar

Pastillage

White satin
shimmer (EA)

Disco white hologram
edible glitter (EA)

Neutral piping jelly

Uncooked spaghetti

Note: letters in brackets refer to suppliers. See Suppliers on pages 152–3.

White sugarpaste

Red jelly sweet

Coloured sugarpaste

Cornflour

Pearl lustre spray (PME)

Food pen

Paste food colourings

**Painting solution
(or clear alcohol)**

Silver dragées/balls (LC)

Sugarpaste

Sometimes referred to as 'fondant' or 'roll-out' icing, sugarpaste is easily bought in sugarcraft shops and supermarkets. It is available in white and many different colours. Using ready-coloured paste can save a lot of time, especially with the darker colours such as red, green or black.

Colouring sugarpaste/royal icing

If you cannot buy readymade sugarpaste in the colour you require, buy white sugarpaste and colour it yourself. Use paste colours for best results as they are more concentrated and give deeper, richer colours. Royal icing can also be coloured with paste colours.

1 Make a hole with your thumb in the middle of the piece of paste to be coloured. Dip a cocktail stick or toothpick into your chosen colour, then put the colour into the hole.

2 Fold the paste over and start to knead the colour in, using icing (confectioner's) sugar to prevent it sticking to the work surface or to your hands. Add more colour as necessary to achieve the colour you require, but take care not to add too much.

Tip

If you wish to colour your own sugarpaste icing, use paste colours in preference to powder or liquid colours. Powder colours can create a grainy effect and liquid colours can change the consistency of your sugarpaste and make it sticky.

Paste colours you will need

Basic colours

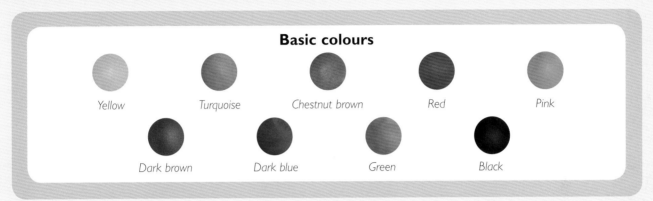

Yellow Turquoise Chestnut brown Red Pink

Dark brown Dark blue Green Black

Mixed colours

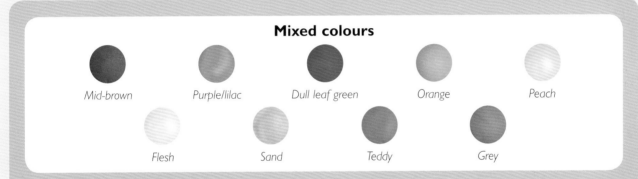

Mid-brown Purple/lilac Dull leaf green Orange Peach

Flesh Sand Teddy Grey

To achieve: Mix:

Mid-brown:	**Chestnut brown and dark brown**
Orange:	**Yellow and red**
Sand:	**Orange, yellow and brown + lots of white sugarpaste**
Purple/lilac:	**Pink and blue**
Peach:	**Pink and yellow + white sugarpaste**
Teddy:	**Orange and brown + white sugarpaste**
Dull leaf green:	**Green and brown**
Flesh:	**Pink and yellow (tiny amounts of each) + lots of white sugarpaste**
Grey:	**Tiny amount of black mixed with white sugarpaste**

Cupcake basics

A basic cupcake recipe

You will need

Makes 24–30 large cupcakes
(24 domed or 30 flatter cakes)

11oz (300g) softened unsalted butter
11oz (300g) caster sugar
6 medium eggs, lightly beaten
11oz (300g) self-raising flour

You can add one of the following for flavour:

1 teaspoon (2.5ml) vanilla extract OR finely grated zest of 2 lemons OR replace 1oz (30g) of the flour with 1oz (30g) unsweetened cocoa powder for a chocolate flavour.

1 Preheat the oven to 170°C/325°F/ Gas mark 3.

2 Line the cupcake tins with cupcake cases.

3 In a large electric mixer, beat the butter and sugar together until the mixture becomes light and fluffy.

4 Add the eggs gradually, beating the mixture well between each addition.

5 Sift the flour, add to the mixture, and mix carefully until just combined.

6 Remove the mixing bowl from the mixer, and fold the mixture gently through with a spatula. Evenly spoon or pipe the mixture into the cases (see page 141).

7 Bake the cupcakes in the oven for about 20 minutes or until a skewer inserted into the centre of one of the cupcakes comes out clean.

8 After baking, sugar syrup can be brushed on to your cupcakes while they are still warm (see recipe opposite). This will make them more moist – but don't add too much because they will become too sticky.

Tip

You can add flavours to the sugar syrup before brushing it on. Pour it over the cupcakes while they are still in the tin, as it is less messy, otherwise transfer the cupcakes to a wire rack to cool.

Sugar syrup recipe

You will need

To soak 25–30 cakes:

5fl oz (150ml) water
5½oz (150g) caster sugar

1 Put the water and sugar in a saucepan and bring to the boil, stirring occasionally. Add any flavours to the syrup at this stage.

2 Allow to cool.

3 Store in an airtight container in the fridge for two to three weeks.

Preparing cupcakes for decoration

Take note of what height and shape of cupcake will suit your design best. Some designs such as the igloo (page 34) require a domed top (bottom left). Others such as the pig (page 71) require a flat-topped cake. You can make a cake that is lower than the top of the case by using less mixture (below, middle) or make a domed cake and cut the top off level with the top of the case (below, right).

A domed-top cupcake.

A low, flat cupcake.

A cut, flat cupcake.

Covering cupcakes

Cupcakes covered with filling cream or royal icing do not have to have a perfectly smooth surface as the icing will hide any imperfections, BUT cupcakes covered in sugarpaste WILL need to have a smooth even surface, so remove any bumps with a small serrated knife before covering.

Flat-topped cupcake

Domed cupcake

Swirl-topped cupcake

Spiky-topped cupcake

Flat-topped cupcake

Cover flat-topped cupcakes with a disc of sugarpaste; stick it in place with apricot purée, or a little filling cream, thinly spread on top.

Domed cupcakes

Brush domed cupcakes with apricot purée and cut a circle of sugarpaste ⅕–⅘in (5–20mm) larger than the top of the cupcake case. Stick it on top and gently smooth it down to meet the edge of the foil case.

Swirl-topped cupcakes

Using a small palette knife, place a generous quantity of either filling cream or royal icing on top of your cupcake. Gently spread it all the way down to the top of the case. Use the tip of your palette knife to create a swirl on top, by starting at the outside and move it inwards in a circular motion.

Spiky-topped cupcakes

Firstly follow instructions for swirl-topped cupcakes and then using the flat underside of your palette knife, pull the icing upwards many times to create lots of pointy spikes.

Decorating cupcakes

How to mark eyes

You will need

Cocktail stick or toothpick
Liquorice black paste food colour

Dip the end of your cocktail stick
into liquorice black paste food colour
and, following the instructions below,
mark the eyes.

Do not mark the eyes as dots. Never
push a cocktail stick into the front of
the face, as this will form a little round
eye and your model will look mean or
unfriendly. This is perfect, however, for
the witch's face, see page 42.

Mark oval or long eyes – rest the black
tip of the cocktail stick against the face
to mark the eyes, and approach the
head at the angle shown in the picture,
to ensure that your eyes are long in
preference to round dots.

Compare the two faces above.
The one with long eyes (right) is
much more friendly and appealing
than the one with dot eyes (left).

How to mark a smile or mouth

1 You can paint a smile with a very
fine paintbrush and black paste colour
slightly diluted with painting solution.

2 You can create an open mouth
by pushing in a pointed tool.

Making a piping bag

1 Cut a piece of greaseproof or silicone paper into a long triangle with one corner cut off. If you are right-handed have this corner on your right, and on the left if you are left-handed.

2 Pick up the right-hand corner and twist it inwards until a tight point is formed in the middle of the long side.

3 Rotate your hand inside until you have rolled to the end of the triangle and your cone is complete.

4 Bend the point of the paper inwards and tuck firmly into the cone.

5 Make a little rip halfway along, then fold over and bend one side inwards – this will secure the bag and stop it unravelling when you let go of it.

6 Fill the bottom half of your bag with peaky royal icing if you are piping hair or grass.

7 If you are adding a piping tube, rip the bottom ⅜in (10mm) off your bag, place the tube inside, then half-fill with royal icing.

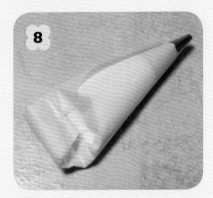

8 Fold the open end of the piping bag over several times to secure the icing inside.

Piping grass and hair

1 Half fill the bag with royal icing. Pinch the pointed end flat between your fingers. Cut the flat end with two snips as shown below. Ensure that both cuts are the same length.

2 Gently squeeze a blob of icing out of the bag, stop squeezing and pull the bag away; you will have formed a little spike.

3 To pipe long grass or witches hair, continue to squeeze along the surface of the cake and only pull away sharply having stopped squeezing when your blade of grass or hair is the correct length.

Piping royal icing with a star tube

These designs are used on the mini cupcake design (see page 98). You will need to practise your piping techniques to perfect the shapes you wish to make, especially as your shells or stars need to be the same size.

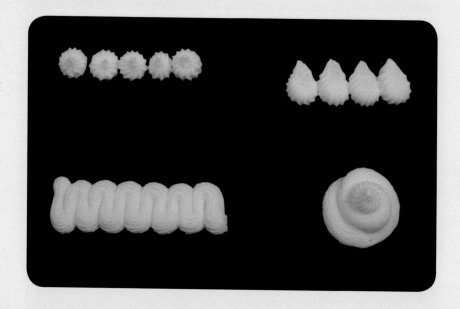

Common mistakes when piping royal icing

• Don't make your royal icing too heavy and stiff – this will make your hand and wrist ache as you are piping. If you find this happens, place your icing back in the mixing bowl, add a little more liquid albumen (egg white), and beat a little more but always on a slow speed to avoid your icing becoming too aerated.

• Don't overfill your piping bag – never fill your piping bag more than halfway for two reasons:

a) You will need a lot more pressure to push the icing out of an overfilled bag, and it will make your hand and wrist ache very quickly.

b) While you are squeezing, the bag will probably start to unravel at the top (wrong) end, and the icing will start oozing out.

How to frill sugarpaste

You will need

Garrett frill cutter
No. 9 modelling tool

1 Cut out your circle with a garrett frill cutter. It should be about ⅛in (2–3mm) thick on a surface dusted with a LOT of icing sugar.

2 Bring your frill to the edge of your smooth flat work surface and roll the fattest part of the modelling tool along the very edge of your frill.

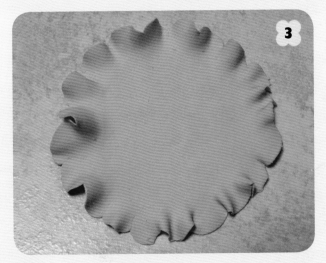

3 Start the next roll along your frill very slightly overlapping the previous one. Continue until you have rolled and frilled all the way around your circle.

Recipes

Making sugarpaste or fondant icing

You can buy ready-made sugarpaste or fondant icing from cake suppliers, but you can easily make your own.

You will need

Makes about 1lb 8oz (675g)

1 egg white
2 tablespoons liquid glucose
1lb 8oz (675g) icing sugar, sifted
A little white fat (optional)

1 Put the egg white and liquid glucose into a bowl and gradually add the icing sugar. Stir until the mixture thickens.

2 Turn out on to a work surface dusted with icing sugar and knead until the paste is smooth and silky. If the paste becomes a little dry and cracked, try kneading in a little white fat.

Filling cream or buttercream

You will need

4oz (115g) unsalted butter or margarine
13oz (375g) icing sugar (confectioner's sugar)
2 tablespoons water

2–4 tablespoons of unsweetened cocoa powder for chocolate buttercream

1 Beat the butter or margarine until it is light and fluffy.

2 Gradually add the water and icing sugar (on a slow speed if using an electric mixer). For chocolate buttercream, add 2–4 tablespoons of unsweetened cocoa powder to the water before it is added to the mixture.

3 Increase the speed of the mixer and continue to beat until the mixture becomes paler and is light enough in consistency to spread easily.

Royal icing

Royal icing is used for piping grass and hair, as well as adding extra detail, such as rows of little piped shells of icing on the Mini Cupcakes (page 98). It is also great for fixing the decorations to your cake.

You will need

Makes about 8oz (225g)

1 egg white
1 teaspoon glycerine
8–9oz (225–250g) icing sugar, sifted

1 Put the egg white and glycerine into a bowl and beat in the icing sugar, a little at a time, until the icing is smooth, white and forms soft peaks when the spoon is pulled out.

2 Cover the bowl with a damp cloth and allow to stand for five minutes to disperse any air bubbles before use.

3 You can store the icing in an airtight container in a cool place, such as a refrigerator, for about ten days. It must be stirred thoroughly before use to bind together all the ingredients once again. If you do not stir thoroughly it will be difficult to work with and will not give a smooth finish.

Apricot purée

Use apricot purée or sugar glue to stick pieces of icing together. Apricot purée is suitable for sticking large pieces and sugar glue for smaller pieces.

You will need

Makes 5fl oz (150ml)

5½oz (150g) apricot jam
2–3 tablespoons water

1 Put the jam and water into a saucepan and heat gently, stirring occasionally, until the jam melts. (It can also be heated in a microwave oven.)

2 Rub through a sieve and allow to cool before using.

Sugar Glue

Apricot purée or sugar glue can be used when sticking pieces of sugarpaste together.

You will need

½oz (15g) simple pastillage
3 teaspoons cool boiled water

1 Break up the pastillage icing in a bowl and pour the water on top. Allow to soak for at least 30 minutes, then mix thoroughly to a thick paste.

2 Sugar glue can be used as soon as it is made. It will keep in an airtight container in the refrigerator for up to ten days.

Pastillage

Pastillage is a sugar-based dough used for making decorations that you want to set rock hard, such as sails (see 'Sailing Boat', page 91). You can buy pastillage from cake suppliers but it is very easy to make your own.

You will need

Makes about 12oz (350g)

1 egg white
2 teaspoons gum tragacanth
12oz (350g) icing sugar, sifted

1 Put the egg white into a mixing bowl. Using 10oz (280g) of the sifted sugar, add to the egg white a little at a time, beating well to make a stiff consistency like royal icing. Level the top and sprinkle the gum tragacanth evenly over the surface. Allow to stand for ten minutes.

2 Turn the pastillage out on a work surface and knead together, incorporating the remaining icing sugar.

3 Lastly, wrap in a polythene bag and store in an airtight container.

Templates

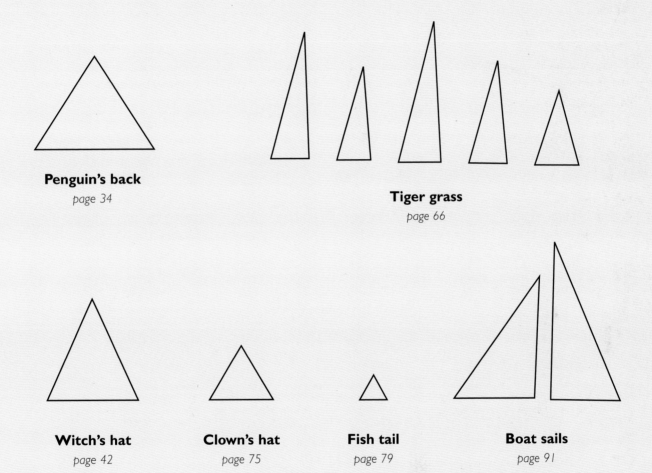

Penguin's back
page 34

Tiger grass
page 66

Witch's hat
page 42

Clown's hat
page 75

Fish tail
page 79

Boat sails
page 91

Suppliers

UK

Ann Pickard (**AP**)
The Icing Centre
26 Nithsdale Road
Weston-Super-Mare
Somerset, BS23 4JR
Tel: +44 (0)1934 624565
www.icingcentre.co.uk
www.annpickardproducts.co.uk

A Piece of Cake
18–20 Upper High Street
Thame
Oxon, OX9 3EX
Tel: +44 (0)1844 213428

COVAPASTE: white sugarpaste

BFP Wholesale Ltd
Unit 8 Connections
Industrial Centre
Vestry Road
Sevenoaks
Kent, TN14 5DF
www.bfpwholesale.com

Culpitt Ltd
Jubilee Industrial Estate
Ashington
Northumberland, NE63 8UQ
Tel: +44 (0)1670 814545
www.culpitt.com

Edable Art (**EA**)
1 Stanhope Close
The Grange
Spennymoor
Co. Durham, DL16 6LZ

Guy Paul and Co. Ltd
Unit 10, The Business Centre
Corinium Industrial Estate
Raans Road
Amersham
Bucks, HP6 6FB
Tel: +44 (0)1494 432121
www.guypaul.co.uk

Lindy's Cakes Ltd (**LC**)
Unit 2, Station Approach
Wendover
Bucks, HP22 6BN
Tel: +44 (0)1296 622418
www.lindyscakes.co.uk

Knightsbridge PME Ltd (**PME**)
Unit 23 Riverwalk Road
(Off Jeffreys Road)
Enfield
Essex, EN3 7QN
Tel: +44 (0)20 3234 0049
www.cakedecoration.co.uk

FPC Sugarcraft (**FPC**)
Hill View
Parfitts Hill
St George
Bristol
Avon, BS5 8BN
www.fpcsugarcraft.co.uk

REGALICE: white and coloured
sugarpaste

Renshawnapier Ltd
Crown Street
Liverpool, L8 7RF
Tel: +44 (0)151 706 8200
www.renshawnapier.co.uk

USA

Beryl's Cake Decorating & Pastry
Supplies
PO Box 1584
North Springfield
VA 22151
Tel: 1-800-488-2749
www.beryls.com

Global Sugar Art
625 Route 3 Unit 3
Plattsburgh
NY 12901
Tel: 1-518-561-3039
www.globalsugarart.com

AUSTRALIA

Cake Decorating solutions
Shop B2, 69 Holbeche Road
Arndell Park
NSW 2148
www.cakedecoratingsolutions.com.au

About the author

Ann Pickard qualified as a baker and cake decorator in 1983 and opened her shop, The Icing Centre, in 1986. She runs a successful cake-decorating business in Weston-Super-Mare Somerset, England, and has published many books on cake decorating, including *Cake Characters* and *Cakes for Occasions* by GMC Publications. She has also produced a range of DVDs on the same subject. Ann also appears regularly on the Ideal World Shopping channel Create and Craft demonstrating her sugarpaste modelling and showing her books.

Acknowledgments

Many thanks to: Renshawnapier for the Regalice sugarpaste used in this book. FPC Sugarcraft for the mini cupcake mould. Dave Pinnock, Carole Erison, and Ruth O'Connell for all their help.

Index

Names of projects are in italics

To place an order, or to request a catalogue, contact:

GMC Publications Ltd

Castle Place, 166 High Street, Lewes, East Sussex, BN7 1XU

United Kingdom

Tel: +44 (0)1273 488005   **Fax:** +44 (0)1273 402866

Website: www.gmcbooks.com